OPEN WOUNDS

Mission: To Proclaim Transformation and Truth
Publisher: Transformed Publishing, Cocoa, FL
Website: www.transformedpublishing.com
Email: transformedpublishing@gmail.com

ISBN: 978-1-953241-63-4

OPEN
WOUNDS

Minister Dorothea Salbi

Dedication

Foremost,
to my daughters
& their daughters.

And to each &
every beloved
daughter of
Our King
(that's you)!

Table of Contents

Introduction

He heals the brokenhearted
And binds up their wounds.
-Psalm 147:3

An open wound that's not taken care of properly can become easily infected. The same is true for open wounds in our hearts from past relationships because we didn't get healed or delivered. That is why they still hunt us today and infect our natural and spiritual lives.

Note from the Author

Open Wounds,
is straight from the heart
and directly to the point.

This book was written
in obedience to God's desire
to share how His heart
mercifully and purposely
heals my heart and is freely
and abundantly available to
perpetually heal your heart too.

A journal component is
included in the back of this
book as an opportunity for
you to honestly address hurt,
experience healing,
and grow in hope & happiness.

She Has No Idea

Her crown needs straightening because she runs without grace. It slides off to the side of her head as she spins.

She skids across the gold-flaked marble floor to a graceful stop, hesitating for a moment before she opens the heavy doors to the throne room.

She enters, running toward her Father, who stands up from His throne when He sees her enter. He steps toward her, extends His arms, and kneels down to her level.

Adjusting her crown to straighten it up, now tilted to the side, from all the things she's been through in life.

He smiles at her with delight and pride. She has no idea what's at the end of the road, around the corner, or down the street.

That's okay. God has designed these crossroads for her to get to the other side. She has no idea, but God does. She has no idea that things are about to shift without her knowing what's going on.

God is about to take her to a place of promises. When a king promises his queen things of a good, blessed, and prosperous life he does everything to make her happy. Take Esther for instance, the king loved her so much he was willing to give her half of his kingdom.

God doesn't want to give her only half, He wants her to enjoy *all* the things in His kingdom He has to offer, which are the fruits of the spirit - love, joy, peace, forbearance, kindness, goodness, faithfulness, self-control, and patience.

She must know who she is, *The Daughter of a King*. Because her father is King she has no worries, nor fear.

For her father is

King

and rules the kingdom,
an excellent King,
a trustworthy King,
& an eternal King.

She knows she is cherished
and protected by
The Most High King,
who is God Almighty.

She knows now that she
can be exactly who she is
-be herself-
because she is unafraid.

Her father has taken her under His wings to show her love that no man has ever shown her. She has no idea that everything she needs will be provided for her, and she has no idea she's part of a royal legacy.

7

Her inheritance is sure, and exceedingly large. She is blessed and highly favored. She is now standing up to straighten her crown because she knows that she is a part of the royal family, a Kingdom with no ending, an eternal Kingdom.

That she is you!
Remember,

He heals the brokenhearted
And binds up their wounds.
-Psalm 147:3

In Psalm 147:3, God reminds us that His power is unlimited. He is mighty enough to heal all wounds no matter when or how they occurred in our lives. Our pain is not beyond His tremendous power.

He is the *Great Physician*, able to reach into our past and heal our soul so our future will not be affected by our past.

1: Mistaken Identity

I was at a point in my life where all hell had broken loose. I didn't even know what I was doing sometimes. Only five months into my marriage, it fell apart.

Woman to woman, some of us prioritize our desire to be loved by a man that we forget to ask God to first show us the man who will love us right. When we make our selection with our natural eyes instead of our spiritual eyes, we are often disappointed.

He who finds a wife finds a good *thing,*
And obtains favor from the Lord.
-Proverbs 18:22

My husband told me he didn't love me like a wife, only as a friend. He also emphasized that he was a man of God.

Funny as I look back over it. *How can a man of God tell his wife that he doesn't love her, after all she had done for him?* Over time, I realized he was a *man of himself.*

He was narcissistic, a people pleaser, loved attention, and wanted people to admire him. Beware of those who are in sheep's clothing, some are really just wolves ready to kill, steal, and destroy your life.

"Beware of false prophets, who come to you in sheep's clothing, but inwardly they are ravenous wolves."
-Matthew 7:15

The thief does not come except to steal, and to kill, and to destroy. I have come that they may have life, and that they may have *it* more abundantly.
-John 10:10

10

Everything that looks good ain't good for you!

My thoughts were consumed with all the things I had done for him, *I am the same woman who was there when you had nothing!*

The more I meditated on the negativity, the more hatred I harbored. I even told him one day, "If I had a gun, I would blow your brains out!"

The hurt was so deep, I was at my breaking point. I cried out to God, "Why is this happening to me? How could he do this?"

Pity party after pity party, then suddenly God spoke, "Be quiet!"

I looked around and He said it again, "Be quiet!"

Awaiting His voice, I got quiet, then He spoke:

> Dorothea, you must take responsibility and accountability for what you allow to happen to you. Can't no one do anything to you unless you allow it and let it happen.

11

All my life I've been hurt in one way or another, never healing from the first hurt. Hurt piled on top of hurt, then covered up with a disguise.

Psalm 147:3 begins with two important words we cannot overlook, *He heals.* Meaning this healing is ongoing. It is not a one-time deal but rather a supernatural act that occurs over and over in the lives of the brokenhearted. As much, and for as long as, we need healing, God's compassion and care are available to us.

I had put everything I had of value into this man. My life was his life, my happiness was his happiness. Around the time I met him, I had just come into some money and spent a lot of it on him.

Wait, let me start from the beginning. The first time I ever saw him was at a church gathering. Mister tall, dark, and handsome to me. Some people who know him might say he wasn't, but let me say this, "Outer appearance is *not* the only thing that makes a

man handsome. What's on the inside has a lot to do with a man's appeal."

Oh yeah, he had me fooled. He opened doors for me and gave me compliments. I fell right over, headfirst in love with him. I wanted to show him that I would be there for him if he needed anything, as his wife. My goal was to be the wife who would never let him down, not intentionally.

We were good until his sister moved in with us. Then he changed quickly. He started complaining about the food I cooked, which was the same food he loved before his sister came. When I asked him what he wanted to eat, he used to reply, "A belly full is a belly full." This man had me fooled from the start.

I withdrew from my family, friends, church family, and most of all God. I knew they were talking about me, *so I thought*. He told anyone who would listen that I didn't cook or clean. Sure enough, the people he talked to knew that was a lie. *How can a man talk about his wife like that to other people; the same woman he said he loved?*

13

I came to find out, *the joke was on me.* His manipulation was calculated. Our relationship was extremely beneficial for him. He was able to get his kids here and his sister who had no place else to go.

No longer will I be a slave to my past. For too long I was a victim, a slave to the emotional pain of my life, involuntarily introduced to me.

I wait quietly before God,
for my victory comes from him.
He alone is my rock and my salvation,
my fortress where I will never be shaken.
-Psalm 62:1-2 NLT

2: Stolen Identity

In the past, I was molested, raped, neglected, used, misused, rejected, battered, and broken. It escalated to the point, I tried to take my own life. My life came to a boiling point, like a pot boiling over on the stove because *you* put too much in it and it has to go somewhere. As a result, it boils over onto the stove, runs down to the floor, then anywhere else it can access.

I realized, my life was *not* mine to take, as I pondered the question, *"How could I take my life when someone gave His life for me, and His name is Jesus?"* I discovered some *new* names for myself, like 'not giving up', 'not giving in', and 'victory'. I would no longer go by my former name 'pity'.

Let me reintroduce myself. My name is Dorothea Jordan. The harm imputed on me left me maimed. I felt as if I had nothing to live for. See, life dealt me a sympathy card, so I played it and followed suit. I didn't want anyone to see me, so I hid behind what everyone expected from me. I ended things I should have continued and held on to things I should have let go. It's funny how the very things we *think* are good for us truly are not. Even when we do know we don't want to admit it.

No longer did I choose to pretend I was okay. As the expression goes, *the cat was out of the bag.* Truthfully, I was struggling. I decided there was no valid reason to continue to pretend or present a different image to

people. I needed help and someone needed to know. I was now willing to admit to people, and more importantly to myself, that I was in pain and distress, something wasn't right.

From the moment I took off my mask of perfection, I began to heal. Not only heal but live. Transformation was taking place. I could be real and honest, which opened the door to find myself again.

Somehow, I had believed I wasn't worthy enough to have the best, so I settled for less. I wanted the marriage I perceived everyone else had, not knowing what was going on behind *their* closed door.

Now, I better understand why God looks at our hearts. We don't have the ability to truly know every facet of a person's heart. People can easily mislead us into thinking one thing, knowing they feel something else.

Deceit and betrayal crushed and hid the woman who God intended for me to be for Him (God). Throughout life, we all experience hurt and pain. We must gather all of *it* and give it to God. In His love, we gain the

17

love that has been there all along, long before any *man* ever came along. I know that now.

Nay, in all these things
we are more than conquerors
through him that loved us.
-Romans 8:37 KJV

3: Reclaimed Identity

God is committed to strengthening us, in Him.

I have learned to never make a choice without checking with God first. Things happen and life goes on, just trust God. He'll never leave you alone. When we put God first, we can never go wrong.

Be strong and of a good courage,
fear not, nor be afraid of them:
for the Lord thy God,
he it is that doth go with thee;
he will not fail thee,
nor forsake thee.

And Moses called unto Joshua,
and said unto him in the sight of all Israel,
Be strong and of a good courage:
for thou must go with this people
unto the land which the Lord
hath sworn unto their fathers to give them;
and thou shalt cause them to inherit it.

And the Lord,
he it is that doth go before thee;
he will be with thee,
he will not fail thee,
neither forsake thee:
fear not, neither be dismayed.
-Deuteronomy 31:6-8 KJV

It is unfruitful and difficult to be in a one-sided marriage, meaning only one spouse truly wants the marriage and the other doesn't. It is *not* going to work.

When the Bible tells us what God has put together, let no man come between, this even means *you*. Sometimes we come between our own marriages.

> ["]Since they are no longer two
> but one, let no one split apart
> what God has joined together."
> -Matthew 19:6 NLT

Let's consider this question: *Who has God joined together?*

Every relationship is not joined together by God. Some have been put together based on the desires of the flesh and some by the influence or suggestion of others. Even simple statements like, "Ya'll look good together", can spark a relationship that later turns into a nightmare. Unless God is in it, *it* won't work.

21

We must realize, *God has to be first in all we do in life.* The first four words recorded in the Scriptures are:

In the beginning God . . .

-Genesis 1:1

So, at the onset of a potential relationship we must consult God.

The enemy targets marriage because he hates unity and togetherness. He brings division cunningly, subtly, and even sometimes boisterously when we allow him to.

I loved my husband. He didn't realize he had in his midst a woman of God. I prayed for him, loved him, cooked for him, cleaned for him, and made love to him.

Most men realize the benefits of having a strong woman as a helpmate, but some prefer women they perceive to be weaker, to manipulate and control.

Always remember, God made us strong. We need to stop chasing people who don't get it, stop pleasing people who are trying to get back into our lives only to contribute further

22

chaos and disturb our peace, and people who God is clearly trying to take out of our lives by showing us who they really are.

I have learned through heartache and tribulations; I can't make anyone love me. I must reserve the *best* me, for who God has for me, instead of further damaging myself trying to *force* a relationship that does not fit. *Let it go!*

We must not allow misuse and mistreatment of the great gift God has made each woman to be to her *own* husband. This is the time in your life to give yourself to God. Allow God to heal you and prepare you for your God-ordained husband. Depend on God, rather than man. Celebrate who God has made you to be and cease grieving those who walked away, abandoned you, forsook you, and left you.

I was married to a 'gaslighter'. Let's look at the definition.

> gaslighting - psychological manipulation of a person usually over an extended period of time that causes the victim to question the validity of their own thoughts, perception of

23

reality, or memories and typically leads to confusion, loss of confidence and self-esteem, uncertainty of one's emotional or mental stability, and a dependency on the perpetrator.[1]

I thank God for the gift of strong faith in those crushing times. Faith in God is what drives us when others give up, surrender, and throw in the towel. Jesus remains faithful, even when we feel faithless.

> If we are faithless, He remains faithful;
> He cannot deny Himself.
> -2 Timothy 2:13

Jesus took care of me when I didn't care for myself. He continues to care for me, and I know He always will. He forever has my back, and He has yours, too.

The Bible warns us to watch out for those who intentionally prey on people, especially in times of vulnerability.

> For of this sort are those who creep
> into households and make captives of
> gullible women loaded down with sins,
> led away by various lusts,
> -2 Timothy 3:6

24

God has really been good to me. We must realize even when we *think* we've lost everything and our life is over, that is not true. Consider those times a new beginning.

It's time to take a stand. Make a quality decision to take your life back. God will tear down every lie and recompense all the wrong that was done to you and make it right.

Recognize, God doesn't need anything that you have lost or anyone who has walked out on you to bless you. God uses what remains to let His presence be known in your life.

I had to come to realize that God is in control of *it* all, at all times. I heard a saying from a movie that has stuck with me, *sometimes we are trying to hold on to things that God is trying to tear apart, because He sees disaster headed our way.*

The Bible tells us that no weapon formed against you or me shall prosper. I'm not saying life is going to be a bed of roses, but what I am saying is, "Don't make life be a bed of thorns by marrying the wrong person."

25

No weapon formed against you
shall prosper, and every tongue
which rises against you in judgment
You shall condemn.
This is the heritage of the servants
of the Lord, and their righteousness
is from Me," says the Lord.
-Isaiah 54:17

Today, I can wholeheartedly say, "God is the head of my life." I will make no decision without first consulting Him. I still struggle with open wounds but just like any other sore this too will heal because Jesus is the ointment who heals. He is the author and finisher of my faith and my life (*see* Hebrews 12:2).

Putting on something new often requires adjustments in self-love and self-respect as we begin to change. We grow into the ways of God, and He suits us for greater in Christ.

---

[1]   "Gaslighting."   Merriam-Webster.com   Dictionary,   Merriam-Webster, https://www.merriam-webster.com/dictionary/gaslighting. Accessed 1 May. 2024.

Bless the Lord, O my soul;
and all that is within me,
bless His holy name!
Bless the Lord, O my soul,
and forget not all His benefits:
Who forgives all your iniquities,
Who heals all your diseases,
Who redeems your life from destruction,
Who crowns you with
lovingkindness and tender mercies,
Who satisfies your mouth with good *things*,
So *that* your youth is renewed like the eagle's.
-Psalm 103:1-5

27

She

She has no crown
because she hasn't found her king,
the man she got is, *Oh, so mean!*

She knows she deserves better,
but she settles for less
going through stormy weather.

She is now getting tired
asking God, *Why?*
as she begins to cry.

God answered her and said,
*Hush my daughter, you're created
from above, I created you to be loved.*

She wiped away her tears
as things became clearer.

She said, *God made me 'help meet'
not a woman to be beat, He made
me strong not to be walked on.*

She has a calling on her life
to be someone's wife,
before you get married
ask God for advice.
By: Dorothea

Closing Remarks

Be the woman who God called *you* to be. A *Proverbs 31 Woman*, who looks for God in all she does, who seeks God first in all her decisions. *Why does a Proverbs 31 Woman put God first?* Because she knows God is her father. She trusts God in all the decisions He makes for her life. With gladness, she will be who God has called her to be to the fullest.

God has called us to be loved, *not* hurt, abused, or used. Take God at His word because He knows what's best. Listen to God and know you are the apple of His eye (*see* Zechariah 2:8).

The heart of this book, I dedicate to my daughters to let them know *not* to give in to or settle for any man who does not love them like Christ loves the church.

Husbands, love your wives,
just as Christ also loved the church
and gave Himself for her[.]
-Ephesians 5:25

31

Also by Minsiter Dorothea Salbi

Not the life I would have picked. Not the life I understood. But it was the life I survived. You can survive, too. Not only can you survive, but you can forgive! *The Shoes I Walked In* were uncomfortable, but I won't complain. Every step I took in those painful shoes, brought me closer to the life of freedom I live today.

Don't delay. You too can walk away from abuse, addiction, abandonment, bondage, & looking for love in all the wrong places.

Author, Dorothea Salbi, authentically shares her story to meet you in your place of pain as an example of courage, grace, love, forgiveness, recovery, and reconciliation. Drugs couldn't stop the pain and people couldn't plug up the void. Dorothea gives all the Glory to the Lord Jesus Christ and desires to share His genuine love with you.

He heals the brokenhearted
And binds up their wounds.
-Psalm 147:3

_____

_____

_____

_____

_____

_____

_____

_____

_____

_____

_____

_____

_____

_____

_____

_____

_____

_____

_____

_____

_____

_____

_____

He heals the brokenhearted
And binds up their wounds.
-Psalm 147:3

_____

_____

_____

_____

_____

_____

_____

_____

_____

_____

_____

_____

_____

_____

_____

_____

_____

_____

_____

_____

_____

_____

_____

_____

_____

He heals the brokenhearted
And binds up their wounds.
-Psalm 147:3

_____

_____

_____

_____

_____

_____

_____

_____

_____

_____

_____

_____

_____

_____

_____

_____

_____

_____

_____

_____

_____

_____

_____

He heals the brokenhearted
And binds up their wounds.
-Psalm 147:3

_____
_____
_____
_____
_____
_____
_____
_____
_____
_____
_____
_____
_____
_____
_____
_____
_____
_____
_____
_____
_____
_____

He heals the brokenhearted
And binds up their wounds.
-Psalm 147:3

He heals the brokenhearted
And binds up their wounds.
-Psalm 147:3

_____
_____
_____
_____
_____
_____
_____
_____
_____
_____
_____
_____
_____
_____
_____
_____
_____
_____
_____
_____
_____
_____
_____
_____
_____

He heals the brokenhearted
And binds up their wounds.
-Psalm 147:3

_____
_____
_____
_____
_____
_____
_____
_____
_____
_____
_____
_____
_____
_____
_____
_____
_____
_____
_____
_____
_____
_____
_____

He heals the brokenhearted
And binds up their wounds.
-Psalm 147:3

_____
_____
_____
_____
_____
_____
_____
_____
_____
_____
_____
_____
_____
_____
_____
_____
_____
_____
_____
_____
_____
_____
_____

He heals the brokenhearted
And binds up their wounds.
-Psalm 147:3

_____
_____
_____
_____
_____
_____
_____
_____
_____
_____
_____
_____
_____
_____
_____
_____
_____
_____
_____
_____
_____
_____
_____
_____

He heals the brokenhearted
And binds up their wounds.
-Psalm 147:3

_____
_____
_____
_____
_____
_____
_____
_____
_____
_____
_____
_____
_____
_____
_____
_____
_____
_____
_____
_____
_____
_____

He heals the brokenhearted
And binds up their wounds.
-Psalm 147:3

_____
_____
_____
_____
_____
_____
_____
_____
_____
_____
_____
_____
_____
_____
_____
_____
_____
_____
_____
_____
_____
_____
_____

He heals the brokenhearted
And binds up their wounds.
-Psalm 147:3

_____

_____

_____

_____

_____

_____

_____

_____

_____

_____

_____

_____

_____

_____

_____

_____

_____

_____

_____

_____

_____

_____

He heals the brokenhearted
And binds up their wounds.
-Psalm 147:3

_____

_____

_____

_____

_____

_____

_____

_____

_____

_____

_____

_____

_____

_____

_____

_____

_____

_____

_____

_____

_____

_____

_____

www.ingramcontent.com/pod-product-compliance
Lightning Source LLC
Chambersburg PA
CBHW070939120626
46546CB00004B/1484